THE SECRET OF SUCCESS

WILLIAM WALKER ATKINSON

SANAGE
PUBLISHING HOUSE

Paperback: 978-811900710-3

Printed by: Mnaipal Technologies Limited, Manipal

Sanage Publishing House LLP
Mumbai, India

sanagepublishing@gmail.com

William Walker Atkinson (December 5, 1862 – November 22, 1932) was an attorney, merchant, publisher, and author, as well as an occultist and an American pioneer of the New Thought movement. He is the author of the pseudonymous works attributed to Theron Q. Dumont and Yogi Ramacharaka.

He wrote an estimated 100 books, all in the last 30 years of his life.

CONTENTS

LESSON I

The Secret Of Success

The Fundamental Rules Of Success. The Instinctive Impulse, How To Succeed. The Leaders Among Men. The Unfoldment Of Individuality.

It is with some hesitation that we bring ourselves to write this little book, entitled "The Secret of Success." Not that we are not in sympathy with the subject not that we do not believe that there is a "Secret of Success", but because there has been so much written on the subject of "Success" that is the veriest twaddle masses of platitudinous wordiness that we hesitate to take the position of a teacher of Success. It is so easy to fill pages of paper with good advice, it is so much easier to say things than to do them so much easier to formulate a code of precepts than to get out into the field of active endeavor and put into practice the same percepts. And you may imagine why we hesitate to assume a role which would lay us open to the suspicion of being one of the "do as I tell you, and not as I do" teachers of the Art of Success.

But there is another side of the question. There is, besides the mere recital of a List of Good Qualities Leading to Success, a list with which every schoolboy and reader of the magazines is acquainted, a Something Else and that Something Else is a suggestion that the Seeker for Success has a Something Within himself which if expressed into activity and action will prove of great value to him, a veritable Secret of Success, instead of a code of rules. And so, we propose to devote this little book to unfolding our idea of what this Something

Within is, and what it will do for one who will unfold it and thus express it into action. So, therefore, do not expect to find this book a "Complete Compendium of Rules Conducive to Success, Approved of and Formulated by the Successful Men of the World who became acquainted with these Rules only after they had Attained Success and consequently had Time and Inclination to Preach to Others." This is not a book of that sort. It is Quite Different. We hope you will like it. It will do you good in any event.

All people are striving and seeking Success. Their idea of Success may differ, but they have all agreed upon the desirability of Attainment. "Attainment", that is the word, which embodies the essence of that which we call Success. It is the "Getting-There" idea, the idea of Attainment of Reaching the Goal for which we set out. That is the story, Attainment.

Many men and women have endeavored to point out the way to Success, and while some have rendered valuable service to those who were following them on the Path of Attainment, yet none have been able to tell the whole story of Success. And this is not to be wondered about, for the reason that on the road to Success each and every individual must be in a measure a law unto himself, or herself. No two temperaments are exactly alike Nature delights in variety; no two sets of circumstances are precisely the same infinite variety manifests here also. And so, it would be folly to attempt to lay down rules of universal application, which would surely lead all to the great goal of Success. One has but to look around him on all sides and see the different needs of the different individuals composing the crowd, in order to recognize the futility of any attempt to lay down lines of universal instruction on this subject. Each and every man who has succeeded has done so in a different way generally along some original lines of action in fact, the faculty or characteristic known as Individuality, seems to have played an important part in the success of the majority of persons who have attained it. And Individuality renders those possessing it to a marked degree to bc likely to depart from any set of rules or laid-out courses of action. And so, it may be stated as a general principle that each must work out his own Success along the lines of his own Individuality, rather than by following any set rule or line of conduct.

In view of what we have just said, it may seem strange that feeling as we do, we have ventured to write a little book entitled "The Secret of Success," particularly as we have started the said book by declaring the impossibility of laying down any set rules on the subject. This may seem like a paradox, but a little examination will show you that it is not so. It is true that we believe that each and every person must work out his own Success, along the lines of his own Individuality, instead of along some cut-and-dried plan. And right here is where the "Secret of Success" comes in. "Along the lines of his own individuality," we have just said then it must follow that one must possess Individuality before he may work along its "lines." And in the measure that he possesses Individuality, so will he possess the first prerequisite to Success. And that is what we mean by "The Secret of Success" Individuality.

Every person possesses dormant and latent Individuality but only a few allow it to express itself. The majority of us are like human sheep trotting along complacently after some self-assertive bellwether, whose tinkling bell serves to guide our footsteps. We have absorbed the notion somehow that these bellwethers possess the sum and substance of human knowledge and power, and ability to think and instead of unfolding our own dormant powers, and latent possibilities, we allow them to remain in obscurity, and we trot along, jogitty-joggity jog after our pet bellwether. People are very much like sheep in this way, they are obedient and imitative animals and rather than assume the responsibility of directing their own footsteps, they wait until someone takes the lead, and then away they stampede after him. Is it any wonder that the leaders claim the choicest pickings for themselves, and allow the flock to get only the scrubby grass? Not a bit of it, they have earned the choice bits by reason of lack of Individuality and Initiative on the part of those following them in fact they were chosen as leaders because of this self-assertive and self-directive quality. If they had stood back in a modest, mild manner, they would have been pushed aside by the flock that would disclaim them as leaders in favor of others who knew how to push to the front.

Now, in this little book we shall not endeavor to awaken a spirit of "bellwetherism" in you, nor to urge you to strive to lead the flock, there is nothing in the mere leading of people other than vainglory and petty self-satisfaction. The desirable thing is to possess sufficient Individuality and Initiative to be your own bellwether to be a law unto yourself, so far as other men are concerned. The great men, the strong men care nothing for the flock, which so obediently trots along after them. They derive no satisfaction from this thing, which pleases only inferior minds, and gratifies only petty natures and ambitions. The big men, the great spirits of all ages have derived more satisfaction from that inward conviction of strength and ability which they felt unfolding into activity within themselves, than in the plaudits of the mob, or in the servility of those imitative creatures who sought to follow in their footsteps.

And this thing called Individuality is a real thing. Inherent in each of us, and which may be developed and brought into activity in each one of us if we go about, it right. Individuality is the expression of our Self that Self which is what we mean when we say "I". Each of us is an Individual and "I" differ from every other "I" in the universe so far as personal expression is concerned. And in the measure that we express and unfold the powers of that "I", so are we great, strong, and successful. We all "have it in us", it depends upon us to get it out into Expression. And this Individual Expression lies at the heart of the "Secret of Success". And that is why we use the term and that is what we shall tell you about in this little book. It will pay for you to learn this "Secret".

LESSON II

The Individual

Individuality and Personality. What the Self really is. What is the Individual which manifests the Power of the Self. The Master in the Brain.

In our last lesson we stated that we considered the "Secret of Success" to consist principally of the Free Expression of the Individual, the "I." But before you will be able to apply this idea successfully, you must first awaken to a realization of what the Individual the "I" within you, really is. This statement may appear ridiculous at first to many of you, but it will pay you to acquaint yourself fully with the idea behind it, for upon the true realization of "I" comes Power.

If you will stop and take stock of yourself, you will find that you are a more complex being than you had at first considered yourself to be. In the first place there is the "I," which is the Real Self or the Individual, and there is the "Me," which is something attached to and belonging to the "I" the Personality. For proof of this, let the "I" take stock of the "Me," and it will find that the latter consists of three phases or principles, i. e. (1) the Physical Body; (2) The Vital Energy; (3) The Mind. Many people are in the habit of regarding their bodies as the "I" part of them, but a little consideration will show them that the body is but a material covering or machine through which and by means of which the "I" is able to manifest itself. A little thought will show that one may be vividly conscious of the "I Am" part of himself while totally oblivious of the presence of the physical body. This being so, it follows that the "I" is independent of the body, and that the latter falls into the "Me" classification. The physical body may exist after the "I" has left it, the dead body is not the "I." The physical body is composed of countless particles which are changing places every moment of our lives our body of today is entirely different from our body of a year ago.

Then comes the second principle of the "Me" the Vital Energy, or what many call Life. This is seen to be independent of the body, which it energizes but it too is transitory and changeable, and readily may be seen to be but a something used to animate and energize the body, an instrument of the "I," and therefore a principle of the "Me". What, then, is left to the "I" to examine and determine its nature? The answer that comes naturally to the lips is, "The Mind, by which I know the truth of what you have just said." But stop a moment, you have said, speaking of the mind, "by which I know" have you not, in saying this, acknowledged the mind to be a something through which the "I" acts? Think a moment, is the mind you? You are aware that your mental states change, your emotions vary, your feelings differ from time to time your very ideas and thoughts are inconsistent and are subject to outside influences, or else are molded and governed by that which you call "I" or your Real Self. Then there must be something behind Mental States, Ideas, Feelings, Thoughts, etc., which is superior to them, and which "knows" them just as one knows a thing apart from itself but which it uses. You say "I" feel; "I" think; "I" believe; "I" know; "I" will; etc.., etc. Now which is the Real Self? The Mental States just mentioned or the "I" which is the subject or Real Cause of the mental phenomena? It is not the Mind that knows, but the "I" which uses the Mind in order to know. This may seem a little abstruse to you if you have never been made a study of the subject but think it over a little and the idea will clearly define itself in your mind.

We are not telling you these things merely to give you an idea of metaphysics, philosophy, or psychology, there are many books that go into these matters at length and in detail, so it is not for that reason. The real reason is that with a realization of the "I" or Real Self, comes a sense of Power that will manifest through you and make you strong. The awakening to a realization of the "I", in its clearness and vividness, will cause you to feel a sense of Being and Power that you have never before known. Before you can express Individuality, you must realize that you are an Individual. And you must be aware of this "I" within you before you can realize that you are an Individual.

The "Me" side of you is what is called Personality, to the outer appearance of yourself. Your Personality is made up countless characteristics, traits, habits, thoughts, expressions, and motions, it is a bunch of peculiarities and personal traits that you have been thinking was the real "I" all this time. But it is not. Do you know what the idea of Personality arose from? Let us tell you. Turn to the pages of any good dictionary and you will see that the word originated from the Latin word "Persona", meaning "a mask used by actors in ancient times", and which the word in turn was derived from two other words, "sonare," meaning to "sound," and "per," meaning "through," the two words combined meaning "to sound through" the idea being that the voice of the actor sounded through the mask of the assumed personality or character. Webster gives the following as one of the meanings of "Person," even to this day: "A character or part, as in a play; an assumed character." So then, Personality means the part you are playing in the Great Play of Life, on the Stage of the Universe. The real Individual concealed behind the mask of Personality is you, the Real Self, the "I" that part of you which you are conscious when you say, "I am," which is your assertion of existence and latent power. "Individual" means something that cannot be divided or subtracted from something that cannot be injured or hurt by outside forces something real. And you are an Individual, a Real Self an "I" Something endowed with Life, Mind, and Power, to use, as you will. A poet named Orr wrote:

> "Lord of a thousand worlds am I,

And I reign since time began,

And night and day, in cyclic sway,

Shall pass while their deeds I scan.

Yet time shall cease ere I find release,

For I am the soul of Man."

LESSON III

Spiritedness

Spiritedness not a fanciful, vague quality, but a real, live, forceful Power in Man. The Assertion of Recognition of Mastery. A wonderful Soul-quality.

To many of you, the title of this lesson Spiritedness may seem to have some connection with "spirits," "disembodied entities," or else the "soul" or some higher part of it, to which the name Spirit is often applied. But, in this case, we use the word in a different sense, and yet in a sense approved by many advanced teachers and investigators of the occult and spiritual. One of the meanings of the word," Spirit", as given by Webster is as follows: "Energy, vivacity, ardor, enthusiasm, courage," etc., while the same authority defines the word "spirited" as: "Animated; full of life and vigor, lively," etc. These definitions will give you a hint of the sense in which we are now using the term, but there is still more to it.

To us the word Spirit expresses the idea of the real essential nature of the Universal Power, and which is also manifested in man as the center of his being his essential strength and power, from whence proceeds all that renders him an Individual. Spiritedness does not mean the quality of being ethereal, "goody-goody," spiritual, otherworldly, or anything of that sort.

It means the state of being "animated," meaning, "possessed of life and vigor" so that the state is really that of being filled with Power and Life. And that Power and Life comes from the very center of one's being, the "I am" region or plane of mind and consciousness.

Spiritedness is manifested in different degrees among different men and even among the animals. It is an elementary, fundamental, primitive quality and expression of Life, and does not depend upon culture, refinement or education, its development seems to depend upon such instinctive or intuitional recognition of the Something Within the Power of the Individual which is derived from that Universal Power of which we are all expressions. And even some of the animals seem to possess it.

A recent writer on the "Taming of Animals" expresses instinctive realization of Spiritedness among some of the higher animals as follows: "Put two male baboons in the same cage, and they will open their mouths, show all their teeth, and 'blow' at each other. But one of them, even though he may possess the uglier dentition, will blow with a difference, with an inward shakiness that marks him as the underdog at once. No test of battle is needed at all. It is the same with the big cats. Put two, or four, or a dozen lions together, and they also, probably without a single contest, will soon discover which one of them possesses the mettle of the master. Thereafter he takes the choice of the meat; if he chooses, the rest shall not even begin to eat until he has finished; he goes first to the fresh pan of water. In short, he is 'king of the cage. 'Now, then, when a tamer goes into a den with a big cat that has taken a notion to act 'funny,' his attitude is almost exactly that of the 'king beast' above mentioned would be toward a subject rash and ill-advised enough to challenge his kingship."

You will notice in the above quotation, that the writer states clearly that it is not always the baboon with the fiercest tusks that is the master, neither does the "king lion" necessarily assert his dominion by winning a physical fight it is something far more subtle than the physical, it is the manifestation of some soul quality of the animal. And so it is with men, it is not always the biggest and strongest physically who rule the ruler becomes so by reason of the mysterious soul quality which we call Spiritedness, and which men often call "nerve," or "mettle," or "sand." When two individuals come into contact with each other there is mental struggle, there may not be even a word uttered and yet soul grapples with soul as the two pairs of eyes gaze into each other, and a subtle something in each engages and grapples with a subtle something in the other. It may be all over in a moment, but the conflict is settled for the time and each of the mental combatants knows that he is victor or defeated, as the case may be. There may be no feeling of antagonism between the parties engaging, but nevertheless there seems to be an inward recognition on both sides that there is something between them that has to be settled at once. The parties may become the best of friends, and yet one of them always leads. And this leadership does not depend upon physical strength, intellectual attainment, or culture in the ordinary sense but upon the manifestation and recognition of that subtle quality that we have called Spirit.

People unconsciously assert their recognition of quality in themselves and others, by their use of the term. We often hear of people "lacking spirit"; being "spiritless"; and of others having had "their spirit broken;" etc. The term is used in the sense of "mettle." A "mettled" horse or man is "high-spirited," according to the dictionaries; and the same authorities define "mettlesome" as "full of spirit," so you see the term is used as we have employed it but the explanation of the source of the "spiritedness" is not given. Breeders of thoroughbred racing horses will tell you that a horse having "spirit" will run a gamer race and will often outdistance and out-wind a horse having higher physical characteristics, but less "spirit" or "class." Horsemen insist that the possession of "spirit" in a horse is recognized by the other horses, who are affected by it and become discouraged and allow themselves to be beaten, although often they may be better racing machines, physically. This spirit is a fundamental vital strength possessed by all living things in degrees and it may be developed and strengthened in oneself. In our next lesson we shall recite a few instances of its manifestation among men.

Oliver Wendell Holmes, in one of his books, gives the following vivid description of the conflict of spiritedness between two men: "The Koh-i-noor's face turned so white with rage that his blue-black mustache and beard looked fearful against it. He grinned with wrath, and caught at a tumbler, as if he would have thrown its contents at the speaker. The young Marylander fixed his clear, steady eye upon him and laid his hand on his arm, carelessly almost, but the Jewel felt that he could not move it. It was no use. The youth was his master, and in a deadly Indian hug in which men wrestle with their eyes, over in five seconds, but which breaks one of their two backs, and is good for three score years and ten, one trial enough settles the whole matter just as when two feathered songsters of the barnyard, game, and dunghill, come together. After a jump or two at each other, and a few sharp kicks, there is an end to it; and it is 'After you, monsieur,' with the beaten party in all the social relations for all the rest of his days."

Fothergill says: "Emily Bronte sketched out her ideal of a being possessed of immense willpower in a thorough ruffian Heathcliff. A massive, muscular brute! Well, it was a girl's conception of a strong man; but I think I have seen some quiet, inoffensive-looking men in spectacles, who could very soon have shown the ruffian where the superiority lay."

A celebrated historical example of Spiritedness, under apparently overwhelming odds, is that of the interview between Hugo, Bishop of Lincoln, and Richard Coeur de Lion, in the church of Roche d'Andeli. In his desire to prosecute the war in Normandy, Richard demanded additional supplies and money from his barons and bishops, but Hugo refused to furnish men or money. He claimed that although the See of Lincoln was legally bound to supply men and money for military service within the four seas of Britain, the war in Normandy did not come under that head, and he defied the king. King Richard, called the Lion-Hearted, was a dangerous man to defy, and so when he summoned Bishop Hugo to Normandy, and the latter went forth to beard the lion in his den, few doubted the outcome, and the bishop's downfall was taken as a matter of course. When the bishop landed in Normandy two friendly barons who informed him that the king was in a terrible rage against him, and who advised him to send some humble, conciliatory message to him before entering the royal presence. But the bishop refused to do this and proceeded boldly to meet his monarch. Richard was sitting at Mass when the bishop entered. Hugo walked up to him and disregarding his frown said, "Kiss me, my lord King!" Richard turned wrathfully away, withholding his salute. But Hugo, gazing into his eyes and shaking the royal shoulder vigorously, repeated his demand. "Thou hast not deserved it," roared the king in anger and chagrin. "I have," retorted Hugo, shaking the royal shoulder the harder. The king gradually dropped his eyes from those of the bishop, and gave the kingly salute and kiss, and the bishop passed on calmly to take part in the service. Hugo afterward defied the king in his council chamber, and persisted in his refusal, and even ventured to rebuke his royal master for infidelity to the queen. The council was astounded, for knowing Richard's courage and fiery temper they expected to see Hugo crush in a moment but instead he emerged the victor in the struggle of Spiritedness. The historian says: "The Lion was tamed for the moment. The King acknowledged nothing, but restrained his passion, remarking afterward, 'If all bishops were like my lord of Lincoln, not a prince among us could lift his head among them.'"

And this was not the first time that this doughty Bishop of Lincoln had vanquished a king. In his earlier days shortly after King Henry Plantagenet had created him bishop, he became involved in a fierce dispute with that monarch. Henry was at Woodstock Park surrounded by his courtiers when Hugo approached. The king feigned not to see the bishop, taking no notice whatsoever of him. After a few moments of strained silence, the bishop, pushing aside a powerful earl who was seated by the king's side, took his place beside the king. The king pretended to be mending his leather glove. The bishop cheerfully and lightly said: "Your Majesty reminds me of your cousin at Falaise." Falaise was the place at which Henry's ancestor Duke Robert met Arlotta, the daughter of a tanner of leather, who bore him his illegitimate son who was afterward known as William the Conqueror. The Bishop's impudent allusion to the king's ancestry was too much for the latter and he was badly worsted in the encounter and later acceded to the wishes of the bishop.

But as Fothergill truly says: "It is a great mistake to suppose that this Will is disposed to air itself on all occasions; far from it. It often has a tendency to conceal itself and is not rarely found under and exterior of much pleasantness. There are men and women, too, who present an appearance of such politeness that they seem to have no will of their own; they apparently exist merely to do what is agreeable to others; but just wait till the time comes, and then the latent will-power is revealed, and we find under this velvet glove the iron hand and no mistake about it. It is the secret of the diplomatist. Talleyrand possessed it to a remarkable degree and was a cool, bold, successful diplomat; Cavour also possessed this power and used it wisely. The blusterer and bragger are devoid of it." It is a subtle, tenuous Power, resting latent beneath the surface and out of evidence but when needed it flashes forth like the dynamic electric spark, driving all before it. It is an elemental force, of irresistible power.

LESSON IV

Latent Powers

The part played by Earnestness, Enthusiasm and Desire. The Manifestation of Will-Power. The Will and what lies behind it.

The majority of you know by actual experience in everyday life that we have within our physical organism that which we call "second-wind." We have essayed some physical tasks, and after a bit found ourselves "winded," that is short of breath, and we are tempted to stop and rest our panting bodies. But we have also found by experience that if we will stick to the task at hand the feeling of physical distress will usually pass away, and we will gain what is called our "second-wind." Now just what this "second-wind" is, is a matter that has long perplexed physiologists and even today they have not been able to hand us down a very good guess at the underlying cause of the phenomenon. It seems to be a fresh start acquired by reason of the opening up of reserve stores of vital energy latent physical power stored away for such emergencies. All persons who have engaged in athletic sports know very well the details of this peculiar physiological phenomenon its actuality is too firmly established to admit any doubt.

And as is often the case, examination shows a curious parallel between the working of Nature on the mental plane and on the physical. Just as there is a physical "second-wind," so is there a mental reserve force or latent energy upon which we can draw and thus get a fresh start. The phenomena attendant upon physical "second-wind," as noted above, is almost exactly duplicated by certain mental phenomena. We may be jaded while performing some tedious bit of mental work, and we begin to feel that we are "all in," when lo! Some new in and away we are off with a full mental "second-wind" doing our work with a freshness, vigor and enthusiasm far surpassing the original effort. We have tapped into a fresh source or supply of mental energy.

The majority of us have little or no conception of the reserve mental energies and forces contained within our being. We jog along at our customary gait, thinking that we are doing our best and getting all out of life that there is in it, think we are expressing ourselves to our utmost capacity. But we are living only in the first-wind mental state, and behind our working mentality are stores of wonderful mental energy and power faculties lying dormant, power lying latent awaiting the magic command of the Will in order to awaken into activity and outward expression. We are far greater beings than we have realized we are giants of power if we did but know it. Many of us are like young elephants that allow themselves to be mastered by weak men, and put through their paces, little dreaming of the mighty strength and power concealed within their organisms.

Those of you who have read our little manual entitled "The Inner Consciousness" will recall what we said therein regarding the regions above and below the plane of the ordinary outer consciousness. And on those hidden planes of the mind, are untold possibilities, the raw materials for mighty mental tasks and achievement, the storage batteries of wonderful accomplishment. The trouble with us is that we do not realize the existence of these faculties. We think that we are merely what we manifest in our ordinary dogtrot gait. Another problem is that we have not had the incentive to take action, we have lacked the interest to do great things, we haven't wanted too hard enough. This "want-to-hard-enough" is the great inciting power in life. Desire is the fire which rouses up the steam of Will. Without Incentive and that means Desire, we accomplish nothing. Given the great, earnest, burning ardent Desire as an animating force, the great incentive to take action, and we are able to get up this mental "second-wind" yes, third, fourth and fifth winds tapping one plane of inward power after another, until we work mental miracles.

We wonder at the achievements of the great men in all walks of life, and we are apt to excuse ourselves by the sad remark that these people seem to "have it in them," while we have not. Nonsense, we all have it in us to do things a hundred times greater than we are doing. The trouble is not in greater than we are doing. The trouble is not in the lack of power and mental material, but in the Desire and Interest, and Incentive to arouse into activity those wonderful storehouses of dynamic power within our mentality, we fail to call into our disposal, and which is like all other natural powers and forces eager and anxious to be manifested and expressed. Yes, that's what we said, "anxious and eager," for all natural forces, penned up and in a static condition seem to be bursting with desire to manifest and express into outer dynamic activity. This seems to be a law of life and nature. Nature and all in it seems to be eager for active expression. Have you not been surprised at yourselves at times, when under some slightly higher pressure and incentive Something Within you seemed to break its bounds and fairly carry you off of your feet in its rush into active work? Have you not accomplished tasks under the stress of a sudden urgent need, that you would have deemed impossible in cold-blood. Have you not carried all before you when you "warmed-up" to the task, whereas your ordinary self would have stood around doing nothing under ordinary circumstances.

Earnestness and Enthusiasm are two great factors in bringing into operation these latent forces, and dormant powers of the mentality. But one need not stand by and wait until you work yourself into a fit of fervor before the energies spring into action. You can by a careful training of the Will or rather, by a carefully training of yourself use your Will manage to get hold of the mental throttle, so that you may pull it down and turn on a full head of steam whenever necessary. And when you have once mastered this, you will find that you are not any more tired when running under full pressure, than when you are crawling along this being one of the Secrets of Success.

To many a person, the term "The Will," means merely a firm, steadfastness of mind, akin to Determination and Fixity of Purpose. To others it means something like Desire. To others, it means "the power of choice," etc. But to occultists, the Will is something far more than these things, it means a Vital Power an Acting Force of the Mind capable of dominating and ruling the other mental faculties as well as projecting itself beyond the mental organs of the individual and affecting others coming within its field of influence. And it is in this sense that we use the word "Will" in this lesson.

We have no desire to take the reader into the dim realms of metaphysics, or even into the lighter but still arduous paths of scientific psychology, but we must acquaint him with the fact of the existence of this thing that we call Will Power and its relation to the "I." Of all the mental faculties or powers, that of the Will is the closest to the "I" or Ego of the person. It is the Sword of Power clasped in the hand of the Ego. One may divorce himself in thought from the other mental faculties and states, but when he thinks of the "I" he is bound to think of it as possessing that power which we call Will. The Will is a primal, original power of the "I" which is always with it until the end. It is the force with which he rules (or should rule) his mental and physical kingdom, the power of which his Individuality manifests itself upon the outside world.

Desire is the great motive power inciting the Will to action in life. As we have shown you the action of Will without the motive power of Desire is unthinkable, and therefore it follows that the culture and right direction of Desire carries with it the channel of expression and manifestation of the Will. You cultivate certain Desires, in order that the Will may flow out along these channels. By cultivating the Desire along certain lines, you are making channels along which the Will may flow in its rush toward expression and manifestation. So be sure to map out your Desire channels clearly by making the proper Mental Images of what you want to be sure and make the Desire channels deep and clear-cut by the force of repeated attention and autosuggestion.

History is filled with examples of men who have developed the use of the Will. We say, "developed the use" rather than "developed Will," for man does not develop his Will, his Will is always there ready for use a man develops his ability to use the Will perfects himself in its use. We have frequently used the following illustration and have not been able to improve upon it. Man is like a trolley car, with the upraised trolley-pole of his mind reaching out to the live wire of Will. Along that wire is flowing the current of Will Power, which it, "taps" and draws down into his mind, and by which he is able to move, and act and manifest power. But the power is always in the Wire, and his "developing" consists in the ability to raise the pole to the Wire, and thus "tap into" its energy. If you will carry this idea in your mind, you will be able to apply this truth more easily in your everyday life.

A great promoter of the steel-pen and electroplating industries, possesses this quality to a marked degree. It has been said of him that: "He had, to begin with a strong, powerful, almost irresistible Will; and whoever and whatever he opposed, he surely conquered in the end." Buxton said: "The longer I live, the more certain I am that the great difference between men, between the feeble and the powerful, the great and the insignificant, is Energy Invincible Determination, a purpose once fixed, and the Victory or Death. That quality will do anything that can be done in this world and no talents, no circumstances, no opportunities, will make a two-legged creature a man without it. In this last quotation and the one preceding it, the idea of Persistence and Determination is identified closely with that of Will. And they are closely identified, the idea being that the Will should be held close, fast, and steadily against the task to be accomplished, just as the steel chisel is held firmly up against the object on the lathe, until its work is accomplished. It is not the mere Determination or Persistency that does the work, these would be of no avail unless the Will were there to do the cutting and shaping. But then again, there is a double-aspect of Will here, the Will in one phase does the work, while in another it forces the mind to hold it up against the task. So, in a sense the Will is the power back of Determination and persistency, as well as the force doing the work, the cutting-edge of the chisel, as well as the firm hand that holds it to its work.

Simpson has said: "A passionate Desire, and an unwearied Will can perform impossibilities, or what would seem to be such, to the cold and feeble." Disraeli said: "I have brought myself by long meditation to the conviction that a human being with a settled purpose must accomplish it and that nothing can resist a Will which will stake even existence upon its fulfillment." Foster says: "It is wonderful how even the casualties of life seem to bow to a spirit that will not bow to them, and yield to sub-serve a design which they may in their first apparent tendency, threaten to frustrate. When a firm, decisive spirit is recognized, it is curious to see how the space clears around a man and leaves him room and freedom." Mitchell has said: "Resolve is what makes a man manifest; not puny resolve; not crude determination; not errant purpose but that strong and indefatigable Will which treads down difficulties and danger, as a boy treads down the heaving frost lands of winter, which kindles his eye and brain with a proud pulse-beat toward the unattainable. Will makes men giants."

So, raise that mental trolley-pole and touch the live wire of Will.

LESSON V

Soul-Force

The Energy of Enthusiasm, and what it really means. What Enthusiasm accomplishes. How to communicate Enthusiasm.

You often have heard the word "Enthusiasm" used, have used it often yourself. But have you ever thought of what the word really means from what source it originated, what is its essential spirit? Few have. The word "Enthusiasm" is derived from the Greek term meaning "to be inspired; to be possessed by the gods, etc.," the term having been originally used to designate the mental state of an inspired person who seems to be under the influence of a higher power. The term originally meant, "Inspired by a superhuman or divine power; ecstasy; etc." It is now used, according to Webster, in the sense of: "Enkindled and kindling fervor of soul; ardent and imaginative zeal or interest; lively manifestation of joy or zeal; etc." The word has acquired a secondary, and unfavorable meaning in the sense of "visionary zeal; imaginative fervor; etc." but its real and primary meaning is that ardent, lively zeal and interest in a thing, which seems to awaken into activity some inner forces of one's nature. Real enthusiasm means a powerful mental state exerted in favor of, or against, some idea.

A person filled with Enthusiasm seems indeed to be inspired by some power or being higher than himself, he taps on to a source of power of which he is not ordinarily conscious. And the result is that he becomes as a great magnet radiating attractive force in all directions and influencing those within his field of influence. For Enthusiasm is contagious and when really experienced by the individual renders him a source of inductive power, and a center of mental influence. But the power with which he is filled does not come from an outside source, it comes from certain inner regions of his mind or soul, from his Inner Consciousness. Those who have read our little manual entitled "Inner Consciousness" will readily understand from what part of the mentality such power is derived. Enthusiasm is really "soul power," and when genuine is so recognized and felt by those coming within its field of influence.

Without a certain amount of Enthusiasm no one ever has attained Success, and never will do so. There is no power in personal intercourse that can be compared to Enthusiasm of the right sort. It comprises Earnestness, Concentration, and Power, and there are a very few people that cannot be influenced in some degree by its manifestation by another. Few people realize the actual value of Enthusiasm. Many have succeeded by reason of its possession, and many have failed by reason of its lack. Enthusiasm is the steam that drives our mental machinery, and which indirectly thus accomplishes the great things in life. You cannot accomplish tasks properly yourself unless you manifest a degree of interest in them, and what is Enthusiasm but Interest plus Inspiration, Inspired Interest, that's what Enthusiasm is. By the power of Enthusiasm, the great things of life are brought to expression and accomplishment.

Enthusiasm is not a thing, which some possess, and others lack. All persons have it potentially, but only a few are able to express it. The majority is afraid to let themselves "feel" a thing, and then to let the "feeling" express itself in powerful action like the steam in an engine. The majority of persons do not know how to get up the steam of Enthusiasm. They fail to keep the fires of Interest and Desire kindled under their mental boiler, and the consequence is they fail to get up the steam of Enthusiasm. Enthusiasm may be developed, by cultivating interest and love of your task. Interest, confidence, and desire arouse Enthusiasm, and it remains for you to either concentrate it so that its effect will be directed straight toward the object, person, or thing that you wish to move, or else allow it to dissipate itself in the air without result. Like steam Enthusiasm may be dissipated or used by concentrated direction it produces results; and by foolish waste and dissipation it fails to do so. The more interest you take in a thing, the greater does your confidence and desire grow and from these arise the steam of Enthusiasm. So, remember always that Interest is the mother of Enthusiasm.

The enthusiastic man naturally tends toward the optimistic frame of mind, and by doing so he diffuses an atmosphere of confident, cheerful expectation around him which tends to inspire confidence in others, and which aids him in his endeavors. He surrounds himself with a mental aura of Success, he vibrates Success and those into whose presence he comes, unconsciously take on his vibrations. Enthusiasm is very contagious, and one filled with the right quality, kind, and degree of it unconsciously communicates his interest, earnestness, and expectations to others. Enthusiasm plays an important part in that which is called Personal Magnetism. It is a live, warm, vital mental quality and it quickens the pulse of the one using it and those who are affected by it. It is different from the cold-blooded indifference that one meets with so often in business, and which causes many a sale to be lost, and many a good thing to be "turned down."

The man who lacks Enthusiasm is robbed of more than half his force of Personal Influence. No matter how good his arguments may be, no matter how meritorious his proposition may be unless he possess the warm vital quality of Enthusiasm, his efforts are largely wasted and his result impaired. Think over the salesmen who have approached you and remember how some of them produced the chilling effect of a damp cellar upon you, while others caused you to sit up and take notice in spite of yourself by reason of their earnest interest and enthusiasm. Analyze the impression produced upon you by the different people with whom you have come in contact, and then see how great an influence Enthusiasm exerts. And then remember the effect it produces upon yourself when you feel it. Enthusiasm is Mental Steam remember that.

A few days ago, there was erected a tablet, in one of the great colleges of the land, as a memorial to a former student in its halls. This young man saved the lives of seventeen people during a great storm on the lake. He swam out after them, one by one, and brought them all in alive. He fainted away from exhaustion and when he recovered consciousness, his first words were, "Boys, did I do my Best?"

The words of this young man express the great question that should urge every true seeker after Success to so live and act that he may be able to answer it in the affirmative. It is not so much a question of "did I do so much," or "did I do as much as someone else?" as it is a matter of "did I do my best?"

The man who does his best is never a failure. He is always a success and if the best should be but a poor pretty thing, still the world will place the laurel wreath of victory upon his brow when he accomplishes it. The one who does his best is never a "quitter," or a "shirker", he stays right on his job until he has bestowed upon it the very best that there is in him to give at that particular time. Such a man can never be a failure.

The man who does his best is never heard asking the pessimistic question, "What's the Use?" He doesn't care a whole lot about that part of it, his mind is fixed upon the idea that he is "on his job," and is not going to be satisfied with anything less than his Best. And when one really is able to answer the great question with an honest, "Yes, I did my Best," then verily, he will be able to answer the "What's the Use" question properly it is "of use" to have brought out the Best work in oneself, if for no other reason than because it is a Man Making process, a developer of the Self.

This infernal "What's the Use" question seems to have been invented by some pessimistic imp of darkness to use in discouraging people making desperate struggles or leading forlorn hopes. It has brought down many a man into the Mire of Despondency and Failure. Chase it out of you mind whenever it appears, and replace it with the question,

"Am I doing my Best," knowing that an affirmative answer settles the other question also. Anything is "Of Use" if it is in the right spirit, in a worthy cause, and because one's own manhood demands it. Yes, even if one goes down to death in the doing of it, still it is a Success. Listen to this story, told in a recent magazine article:

It is a story of a sailor on the wreck of a German kerosene steamer, which dashed against the rocks of the Newfoundland coast in the early part of 1901. She had taken fire and had been run ashore on a submerged reef about an eighth of a mile from the coast. The coastline itself was a wall, some four hundred feet high. When morning dawned, the fishermen on shore saw that her boats were all gone and all the crew and officers had apparently been lost, all except three men. Two of these three men were standing on the bridge the third was aloft, lashed to the rigging. Later, the watchers saw a tremendous wave strike the vessel, sweeping away the bridge and the two men who had been standing on it. Several hours later they saw the man in the rigging unlash him and beat his arms against his body vigorously, evidently to restore the circulation, which had been almost stopped by the lashing and the extreme cold. The man then took off his coat, waved it to the fishermen on top of the cliff and then plunged into the sea. The first thought was that he had given up the fight and committed suicide, but he was not that kind of a man. He struck out for shore, and reaching it made three separate attempts to secure a foothold on the rocks at the bottom of the cliff. But he failed three times was he swept away by the surf, and finally, seeing the futility of his efforts, he swam away again, toward the ship. As the narrator well says: "At that crisis in the struggle ninety-nine men out of a hundred would have given up and allowed themselves to drown but this man was not a quitter."

After a fierce battle with the waves the man gained the ship, and after a desperate struggle managed to board her. He climbed again into the rigging and waved his hand to the fishermen high up on the cliff, who were unable to help him. He lashed himself fast, and until dark could be seen signaling the fishermen above, to show them that he was still alive and game. When the following morning broke the fishermen saw that his head had fallen to his breast, he was motionless frozen during the night. He was dead, his brave soul had gone forth to meet its maker, and who can doubt that when that man confronted his Maker his eyes were looking firmly and bravely toward the Presence, and not bowed down in shame or fear. Such a man was indeed worthy to face his Maker, unabashed and unashamed. As the writer, George Kennan, has said in words that make one thrill: "That man died as a man in adverse circumstances ought to die, fighting to the last. You may call it foolish and say that he might better have ended his sufferings by allowing himself to drown when he found that he could not make a landing at the base of the cliff but deep down in your hearts you pay secret homage to his courage, his endurance, and his indomitable will. He was defeated at last, but so long as he had consciousness neither fire nor cold, not tempest could break down his manhood."

The Caucasians have a favorite proverb that says: "Heroism is endurance for one moment more." And that one moment more tells the difference between the "quitter" and the man who has "done his Best." No one is dead until his heart has ceased beating and no one has failed so long as there is one more bit of fight in him. And that "one moment more" often is the moment in which the tide turns, the moment when the enemy relaxes his hold and drops back beaten.

LESSON VI

The Power of Desire

The Motive Force that runs the world. A useful servant but a poor master. How to Create Desire. How to apply its wonderful Energy. How to extend the Mind Force by Desire.

What is Desire? Let us see! Webster tells us that it is: "The natural longing to possess any seeming good; eager wish to obtain or enjoy," or in its abnormal or

degenerate sense: "excessive or morbid longing; lust; appetite." "Desire" is a much-abused term, the public mind has largely identified it with its abnormal or degenerate phase, just mentioned, ignoring its original and true sense. Many use the word in the sense of an unworthy longing or craving, instead of in the true sense of "aspiration," "worthy craving and longing," etc. To call Desire "aspiration" renders it none the less Desire. To apply to it the term "laudable aim and ambition" does not take away from it is character of Desire. There is no sense in endeavoring to escape the fact that Desire is the natural and universal impulse toward action, be the action good or bad. Without Desire the Will does not spring into action, and nothing is accomplished. Even the highest attainments and aims of the race are possible only when the steam of Will is aroused by the flame and heat of Desire.

Some of the occult teachings are filled with instructions to "kill out desire," and the student is warned to beware of it even in its most insidious and subtle forms, even to the extent of "avoiding even the desire to be desireless even desire not to desire." Now this is all nonsense, for if one "wishes," or "wants," or "is inclined," or "thinks best to," or "is pleased to" Kill Out Desire in any of these cases he is but manifesting a Desire "not to desire," in spite of his use of other names. What is this "wishing to; wanting to; feeling like; inclination; being pleased to;" and all the rest but just plain, clear, unadulterated Desire masquerading under some of these names. To proceed to "kill out desire" without "desiring" to do so is like trying to lift oneself by pulling on his own bootstraps. Folly. What is really meant is that the occultist should proceed to kill out the lower desires that he finds within his nature and also to kill out the "attachment" for things. Regarding this last we would say that all true occultists know that even the best "things" are not good enough to rule and master one, nothing is good enough for the soul to allow itself to be unduly attached to it so that the thing rules the soul instead of the soul mastering the thing. That is what the teachings mean avoidance of "attachment." And in this the occult teachers are clearly right. Desire is a frightful master like fire it sweeps away the supports of the soul, leaving nothing but smoldering ashes. But, also like Fire Desire is a splendid servant and by its harnessed power we are able to generate the steam of the Will and Activity, and to accomplish much in the world. Without proper Desire the world would be without activity. So do not make the mistake of using Desire any more than you would refuse to use fire but, in both cases, keep the mastery in your own hands and avoid allowing the control to pass from you to Desire.

Desire is the motivating force that runs the world as little as we care to admit it in many cases. Look around you and see the effects of Desire in every human act, good or bad. As a writer has said: "Every deed that we do, good or bad, is prompted by Desire. We are charitable because we Desire to relieve our inner distress at the sight of suffering; or from the Desire of sympathy; or from the Desire to be respected in this world, or to secure a comfortable place in the next. One man is kind because he Desires to be kind because it gives him satisfaction to be kind, while another man is cruel from precisely the same kind of motive. One man does his duty because he Desires to do it, he obtains a higher satisfaction from duty well done than he would from the neglecting of it in accordance with some weaker desires. The religious man is religious because his religious desires are stronger than his irreligious ones because he finds a higher satisfaction in religion than in the pursuits of the worldly-minded. The moral man is moral because his moral desires are stronger than his immoral ones, he obtains a greater satisfaction in being moral than in being the contrary. Everything we do is prompted by Desire in some shape or form high or low. Man cannot be Desireless and act in any way. Desire is the motivating power behind all actions, it is a natural law of life. Everything from the atom to the monad; from the monad to the insect from the insect to man; from man to Nature, acts and does things by reason of the power and force of Desire, the Animating Motive."

All the above at the first glance would seem to make of man a mere machine, subject to the power of any stray desire that might happen to come into his mind. But this is far from being so. Man acts not upon Every desire, but upon the Strongest Desire, or the Average of his Strongest Desires. This Average of Desires is that which constitutes his Nature or Character. And here is where the Mastery of the "I" comes in! Man need not be a slave or creature of his Desires if he will assert his Mastery. He may control, regulate, govern, and guide his Desires in any directions that he pleases. Nay, more, he may even Create Desires by an action of his Will, as we shall see presently. By a knowledge of psychological laws, he may neutralize unfavorable Desires, and grow and develop yes, practically Create New Desires in their place, all by the power of his Will, aided by the light of his Reason and Judgment. Man is the Master of his Mind.

"Yes," but some close reasoning critic may object; "yes, that is true enough, but even in that case is not Desire the ruling motive must not one Desire create these new Desires before he can do so is not Desire always precedent to action?" Very close reasoning this, good friends, but all advanced occultists know that there is a point in which the Principle of Desire shades and merges into its companion Principle, Will, and that a close reasoner and mental analyst may imagine a mental state in which one may be almost said to manifest a Will to Will, rather than to merely Desire to Will. This state must be experienced before it can be understood, words cannot express it.

We have stated that it was in the power of man to Create Desire, not only to be its master when created, but also to actually Create it by bringing it into being. And the statement is absolutely true and is verified and proven by the most recent experiments and discoveries of modern psychology. Instead of man being a creature of Desire and this indeed he is in many cases, he may become Master of Desire and even a Creator of it. By knowledge and Will he may reverse the ordinary order of things and, displacing the intruder from the throne, he may seat himself there in his rightful place and then bid the late occupant do his will and obey his bidding. But the best way for the new occupant of the throne to bring about a reorganized court is to dismiss the old objectionable creatures of his mind and create new ones in their places. And here is how it may be done:

In the first place, one must think carefully over the tasks that he wishes to accomplish, then, using his judgment carefully, judicially, and impartially, impersonally so far as is possible he must take mental stock of himself and see in what points he is deficient, so far as the successful accomplishment of the task is concerned. Then let him analyze the task before him, in detail, separating the matter into as many clearly defined divisions as possible, so that he may be able to see the Thing as It Is, in detail as well as in its entirety. Then let him take a similar inventory of the things, which seem necessary of the accomplishment of the task not the details that will arise only as the work progresses, day by day but the general things, which must be done in order that the task is brought to a successful conclusion. Then having taken stock of the task, the nature of the undertaking, and one's own qualifications and shortcomings then Begin to Create Desire, according to the following plan:

The first step in the Creation of Desire is that of the forming of a clear, vital Mental Image of the qualities, things, and details of the undertaking, as well as of the Completed Whole. By a Mental Image we mean a clear-cut, distinct mental picture in the Imagination of the things just named. Now, do not turn away with an impatient motion at the mention of the word Imagination. That is another word that you have only a mistaken idea of. Imagination means far more than the mere idle, fanciful use of that part of the mind that is believed by people to be "all there is to it." It isn't all, by a long way in fact, the fanciful part may be said to be merely a shadow of the real Imaginative effort. Imagination is a real thing, it is a faculty of the mind by which it creates a matrix, mold, or pattern of things, which the trained Will and Desire afterward, materializes into objective reality. There has been nothing created by the hands and mind of man which did not have its first origin in the Imagination of someone. Imagination is the first step in Creation, whether of worlds or trifles. The mental pattern must always precede the material form. And so, it is in the Creation of Desire. Before you can Create a Desire, you must have a clear Mental Image of what you need to Desire.

You will find that this task of creating a Mental Image is a little harder than you had expected at the start. You will find it hard to form even a faint mental picture of that which you need. But be not discouraged and persevere for in this, as everything else. Practice makes perfect. Each time you try to form the Mental Image it will appear a little clearer and more distinct, and the details will come into a little more prominence. Do not tire yourself at first but lay aside the task until later in the day, or tomorrow. But practice and persevere and you will soon be able to See Mentally the things you need, just as clearly as a memory picture of something you have already seen. We shall have more to say on this subject of Mental Imagery and Imagination in subsequent lessons.

Then, after having acquired the clear Mental Image of the things you wish to Desire, and thus attain, cultivate the focusing of the Attention upon these things. The word attention is derived from the Latin word "Attendere," meaning "to stretch forth," the original idea being that in Attention the mind was "stretched forth," or "extended" toward the object of attention, and this is the correct idea for that is the way the mind operates in the matter. Keep the ideas before your attention as much as possible, so that the mind may take a firm grasp upon them and make them a part of itself by doing this you firmly impress the ideas upon the wax tablet of the mind.

Thus, having fixed the idea clearly in your mind, by means of the Imagination and Attention, until as we have said, it becomes a fixture there, begin to cultivate an ardent Desire, Longing, Craving Demand for the materialization of the things. Demand that you grow the qualities necessary for the task, demand that your mental pictures materialize Demand that the details be manifested as well as the Whole, making allowance for the "something better" which will surely arise to take the place of the original details, as you proceed the Inner Consciousness will attend to these things for you.

Then Desire firmly, confident, and earnestly. Be not half-hearted in your demands and desires, claim, and demand the Whole Thing and feel confident that it will work out into material objectivity and reality. Think of it, dream of it and always long for it, you must learn to want it the worst way learn to "want it hard enough." You can attain and obtain many things by "wanting them hard enough", the trouble is with most of us that we do not want things hard enough, we mistake vague cravings and wishes for earnest, longing demanding Desire and Want. Get to Desire and Demand the Thing just as you demand and Desire your daily meals. That is "wanting it the worst way." This is merely a hint, surely you can supply the rest, if you are in earnest, and "want too hard enough."

LESSON VII

The Law of Attraction

Nature's Great Law. From Atom to Man. How to draw to us the things we Desire or Fear. Desire Force. How to cultivate and master this great power of the Mind. Fear thought, and how to overcome it.

There is in Nature a great Law, the Law of Attraction by the operations of which all things from atoms to men are attracted toward each other in the degree of the common affinity of common use. The reverse of this law which is merely another manifestation of its power is what is called Repulsion, which is but the other pole of Attraction, and by the operations of which things tend to repel each other in the degree that they are unlike, opposing, and of no use to each other. The Law of Attraction is Universal, on all the planes of life, from the physical to the spiritual. Its operations are uniform and constant, and we may take the phenomena of one plane and thereby study the phenomena of another plane, for the same rule applies in each case, the same Law is in operation in the same way.

Beginning with the tiny corpuscles, electrons, or ions of which the atoms are formed, we find manifested the Law of Attraction, certain electrons attract each other and repel others still, thereby causing to spring into existing groups, combinations and colonies of electrons which being in agreement and harmony manifest and constitute what are called atoms, which until recently were supposed to be the primal form of matter. Passing on the atoms themselves, we find many degrees of affinity and attraction existing between them which cause them to combine and form into molecules of which all masses of matter consists of. For instance, every drop of water is composed of countless molecules of water. And each molecule is composed of two atoms of Hydrogen and one atom of Oxygen, the combination always being the same in every molecule of water. Now, why do these atoms combine in just this way, the same invariable grouping and proportion? Not by chance, surely, for there is no such thing in Nature, there is a natural law back of every phenomenon. And in this case, it is the Law of Attraction manifesting in the case of these atoms. And it is so in all chemical combinations, it is called Chemical Affinity. Sometimes an attached atom will come in contact with or in proximity to another atom and then bang goes the explosion of the molecule as the atom flies away from its partners and into the arms of the other atom for which it has a greater affinity. There are marriages and divorces in the world of atoms, you will notice.

And in the cases of the molecules, it is found that certain molecules are attracted to others of the same kind, under what is called Cohesion, and thus masses of matter are composed. A piece of gold, silver, tin, glass, or other forms of matter is composed of countless molecules held together tightly by Cohesion and this Cohesion is merely another form of the Law of Attraction, the same that draws all things together. And underlying the Law of Attraction is to be found our old Principle of Desire and Will. You may shrug your shoulders at this mention of desire and Will in connection with electrons, atoms, molecules, all forms of matter but just wait a bit and see what the leading scientific authorities have to say on the subject.

Prof. Hakel, one of the world's greatest scientists, a materialist who would sneer at the teachings of Mental Science even this man, naturally prejudiced against mentalist theories, finds himself compelled to say: "The idea of chemical affinity consists in the fact that the various chemical elements perceive the qualitative differences in other elements, experience pleasure or revulsion at contact with them and execute specific movements on this ground." He also positively and distinctly states that in the atoms there must be something corresponding to Desire for contact and association with other atoms, and Will to enable the atom to respond to the Desire. Law is constant throughout Nature, from atom to man physical, mental, and spiritual.

But what has all this to do with the Secret of Success you may ask? Simply, that the Law of Attraction is an important part in the Secret of Success, inasmuch as it tends to bring to us the things, persons, and circumstances in accordance with our earnest Desire, Demand and Will, just as it brings together the atoms and other particles of matter. Make yourself an atom of Living Desire and you will attract to yourself the person, things and circumstances fitting in with the accomplishment of your Desire. You will also get into rapport with those who are working along the same lines of thought and will be attracted to them and they to you, and you will be brought into relations with persons, things, and environments likely to work out the problem of your Desires, you will get "next to" the right persons and things, all by the operation of this great natural Law of Attraction. No Necromancy or Magic about it at all, nothing supernatural or mysterious just the operations of a great Natural Law.

You can do little by yourself in Life, be ever so strong and able. Life is a complex thing and individuals are interdependent upon each other for the doings of things. One Individual, segregated from all the other Individuals, could accomplish little or nothing along the lines of outer activity. He must form combinations, arrangements, harmonies, and agreements with others and in accordance with environments and things, that is, he must create and use the proper environments and things and draw to himself others with whom he must form combinations, in order to do things. And these persons, things and environments come to him and he to them by reason of this great Law of Attraction. And the way he sets into operation this great Law of Attraction is by the operation of his Desire, and along the lines of Mental Imagery. Do you see the connection now? So be careful to form, cultivate and manifest the right Desires hold to them firmly, strongly, and constantly, and you will set into operation this great Law, which forms an important part of the Secret of Success.

Desire-Force is the motive power leading the activities of Life. It is the basic vital power, which animates the minds of living things and urges them forth to action. Without strong Desire no one accomplishes anything worthy of the name and the greater the desire the greater will be the amount of energy generated and manifested, everything else being equal. That is to say, that given a dozen men of equal intellect, physical health, and mental activity equal in everything else except Desire, in short, the ones in whom the greatest Desire resides and is manifested will outstrip the others in attainment and of these winners the one in who Desire burns like an unquenchable flame will be the one who will Master the others by the force of his primitive elementary power.

Not only does Desire give to the man that inward motive which leads to the enfoldment of the power within himself, but it does more than this; it causes to radiate from him the finer and more subtle mental and vital forces of his nature, which, flowing forth in all directions like the magnetic waves from the magnet or the electric waves from the dynamo, influencing all who come within the field of force. Desire-Force is a real, active, effective force of Nature, and serves to attract, draw, and bring to a center that which is in line with the nature of the Desire. The much talked of Law of Attraction, of which so much is heard in Mental Science and the New Thought, depends largely upon the force and power of Desire. Desire-Force is at the center of the Law of Attraction. There is a tendency in Nature to attract and draw to the center of a Desire the things, which are needed to fulfill that, Desire. One's "own will come to him" by reason of his natural force, which lies behind and underneath the entire phenomena of Mental Influence. This being so, does it not become at once apparent why one who wishes to accomplish anything should be sure to create a strong Desire for it and at the same time be sure to acquire the art of Visualization so as to form a clear Mental Picture of the thing Desired, a clear mold in which the materialized reality may manifest?

Have you ever come in contact with any of the great men of modern business life? If you have seen these people in action, you will have become conscious of a subtle, mysterious something about them, a something that you could actually feel, a something that seemed to draw you to fit in to their schemes, planes, and desires almost by an irresistible force. These people are all people of the strongest kind of desire, their Desire Force manifests strongly and affects those with whom they come in contact. Not only this but their Desire-Force flows from them in great waves, which occultists inform us soon manifests a circular or whirlpool-like motion, swing around and around the center of the Desire, these men become actual cyclones of Desire into which nearly everything that comes within its sweep is affected and swept into the vortex. Have we not evidences of this in the cases of all the great leaders of men, can we not see the operation of that mighty law of attraction which brings to them their own? We are apt to call this Will Power and so it is in a way, back and under the Will in such cases is to be found the ardent, burning Desire that is the motive force of the attractive power.

This Desire-Force is a primitive, elemental thing. It is found in the animal kingdom and among the lower races of men, perhaps more clearly than among the higher types of men, but only because in such instances it is seen stripped of the covering, sheaths, disguises, and masks that surround the more civilized forms and planes of life. But remember this well, the same principle is manifested under and beneath the polished veneer of civilized life, the Desire-Force of the cultured leader of men is as elemental as that animating the fierce and shaggy caveman or the wild Berserker who, naked and half-mad, rushed upon overwhelming hordes of his enemy, brushing them aside like flies that is, if you will but look beneath the polished surface. In the old wild days Desire manifested its force on the physical plane, now it manifests on the Mental Plane that is the only difference, the Force is the same in both cases.

While we write, there has just been produced on stage a new play that illustrates this principle. The heroine, the daughter of an old New York family of high social standing and wealth, has a dream of her life in a former incarnation, in which she sees herself torn from the arms of her cave-dweller father by the mighty arms of a fierce savage chief, whose desire is manifested through the physical. She awakens from her dream, and to her horror soon discovers the face of her dream-captor on a man who comes into her father's life in New York. This man comes from the West, forceful, resourceful, and desirous, beating down all before him in the game of finance. As of old, he places his foot on the neck of his enemies but on the mental-plane, this time, instead of the physical. The same old Desire for power is strong within him, the same old masterfulness manifests itself. This man says: "I have never quit; I have never been afraid." The same old Desire then flamed up in the savage now manifests in the Master of Wall Street and between the force of its Attraction and the coupled and allied force of his Will, he repeats the performances of his previous incarnation but on the plane of mental forces and achievement this time mind, not muscle, being the instrument through which the Desire manifests.

We give the above example merely as an illustration of the fact that Desire is the motivating force that moves the Will into action, and which cause the varied activity of life, men, and things. Desire-Force is a real power in life and influences not only the powers and achievement of oneself but also attracts, influences, and compels other persons and things to swing in toward the center of the desire sending forth the currents. In the Secret of Success, Desire plays a prominent part. Without a Desire for Success, there is no Success, none. The Law of Attraction is set into motion by Desire. The majority of the principles advanced in this book have been in the nature of Positive injunctions that is, you have been urged to do certain things rather than to not do the opposite or contrary. But here we come to a place in which the advice must be given along the negative lines, we must urge you not to do a certain thing. We allude to that great poison of the mind and will known as Fear. We do not allude to physical fear important though physical courage may be, and as regrettable as physical cowardice may be considered, still it is not a part of the purpose of this book to preach against the latter and advise a cultivation of the former quality, you will find much of that elsewhere. Our purpose here is to combat that subtle, insidious enemy of true Self-Expression which appears in the shape and guise of mental fear, forebodings which may be considered as Negative Thought just as the other principles mentioned in this work may be considered as Positive Thought.

Fear thought is that condition of the mind in which everything is seen through blue glasses in which everything seems to bring a sense of the futility of endeavor the "I Can't", principle of mentality, as contrasted with the "I can, and I Will" mental attitude. It is the noxious weed in the mental garden, which tends to kill the valuable plants to be found therein. It is the fly in the ointment, the spider in the cup of the Wine of Life. So far as we know the first person to use the word "Fear thought", which has now passed into common use was Horace Fletcher, the well-known writer, who coined it to supplant the use of the word "Worry" in a certain sense. He had pointed out that Anger and Worry were the two great hindrances to a well-balanced, advanced, and progressive mentality, but many misunderstood him and urged that to abolish Worry meant to cease taking any consideration of the morrow, a lack of common prudence and forethought. And so, Fletcher coined the word "Fear-thought" to express a phase of his idea of "Forethought without Worry," and he entitled his second book on the subject, "Happiness, as found in Forethought minus Fear-thought," a very happy expression of a very happy idea. Fletcher also was the first to advance the idea that Fear was not a thing-in-itself, but merely an expression of Fear-thought, a manifestation of the state of mind known as Fear-thought. He and others who have written on the subject, have taught that Fear might be abolished by the practice of abolishing Fear-thought from the mind by driving it out of the mental chamber and the best teachers have taught that the best way to drive out Fear (or any other undesirable mental state) was by cultivating the thought of the opposite quality of mind by compelling the mind to dwell upon the mental picture of the desirable quality, and by the appropriate auto-suggestions. The illustration has often been stated that the way to drive darkness from a room is not to shovel it out, but to throw open the shutters and let the sunlight stream in and that is the best way to neutralize Fear-thought.

The mental process has aptly been spoken of as "vibrations," a figure that has a full warrant in modern science. Then, by raising the vibration to the Positive pitch, the negative vibrations may be counteracted. By cultivating the qualities recommended in the other lessons of this book. Fear-thought may be neutralized. The poison of Fear-thought is insidious and subtle, but it slowly creeps through the veins until it paralyzes all useful efforts and action, until the heart and brain are affected and find it difficult to throw it off. Fear-thought is at the bottom of the majority of failures and "going down" in life. As long as a man keeps his nerve and confidence in himself, he is able to rise to his feet after each stumble and face the enemy resolutely but let him feel the effects of Fear-thought to such an extent that he cannot throw it off and he will fail to rise and will perish miserable. "There is nothing to fear except Fear," has well been said.

We have spoken elsewhere about the Law of Attraction, which operates in the direction of attracting to us, that which we Desire. But there is a reverse side to this, it is a poor rule that will not work both ways. Fear will set into motion the Law of Attraction just as well as Desire. Just as Desire draws to one the things he pictures in his mind as the Desired Thing, so will Fear draw to him the thing pictured in his mind as the Thing Feared. "The thing that I feared hath befallen me." And the reason is very simple, and the apparent contradiction vanishes when we examine the matter. What is the pattern upon which the Law of Attraction builds under the force of Desire? The Mental Image, of course. And so, it is in the case of fear the person carries about the Mental Image or haunting picture of the Feared Thing, and the Law of Attraction brings it to him just as it brings the Desired Thing. Did you ever stop to think that Fear was the negative pole of Desire? The same laws work in both cases.

So, avoid Fear-thought as you would the poisonous draught that you know would cause your blood to become black and thick, and your breathing labored and difficult. It is a vile thing, and you should not rest content until you have expelled it from your mental system. You can get rid of it by Desire and Will, coupled with the holding of the Mental Image of Fearlessness. Drive it up by cultivating its opposite. Change your polarity. Raise your mental vibrations. Someone has said, "There is no Devil but Fear", then send that Devil back to the place where he properly belongs, for if you entertain him hospitably, he will make your heaven a hell in order that he may feel at home. Use the mental Big Stick on him.

LESSON VIII

Personal Magnetism

The Rationale of Personal Magnetism. What it is and what it does. How it affects others. The magnetic attraction manifested by certain people.

We hear much about Personal Magnetism these days. It is a peculiar quality of the mental being of the individual that serves to bring other persons into a mood or state of mind sympathetic with that of the magnetic person. Some men have this quality developed to a wonderful extent and are able to bring about a harmonious agreement on the part of other persons in a short time, while others are almost entirely deficient in this respect and their very presence tends to arouse antagonism in the minds of others. The majority of people accept the idea of Personal Magnetism without question, but few will agree upon any theory attempting to account for it.

Those who have studied the matter carefully know that the whole thing depends upon the mental states of the individual, and upon his ability to cause others to "catch" his mental vibrations. This "catching" is caused by what is known as Mental Induction. Induction, you know, is "that property or quality, or process by which one body having electrical or magnetic polarity produces it in another without direct contact." And Mental Induction is a manifestation of similar phenomena on the mental plane. People's mental states are "catching" or "contagious," and if one infuses enough life and enthusiasm into his mental state's, they will affect the minds of persons with whom they come in contact. We have explained this matter in detail in the little book of this series entitled, "Mental Influence."

It seems to us that the prime factor in successful Mental Induction or manifestations of Personal Magnetism is Enthusiasm. In another lesson in this book, we have told you about Enthusiasm, and when you think of Personal Magnetism, it will be well for you to read what we have said about Enthusiasm also. Enthusiasm gives Earnestness to the person, and there is no mental state so effective as Earnestness. Earnestness makes itself felt strongly and will often make a person give you attention in spite of himself. Walter D. Moody, a well-known writer on the subject of Salesmanship, says, truthfully, "It will be found that all men possessed of personal magnetism are very much in earnest. Their intense earnestness is magnetic." And nearly every student of the subject has noted this fact. But the earnestness must be more than a firm, confident, honest belief in the thing being presented to the attention of the other person. It must be a live, contagious earnestness, which can best be described as Enthusiasm. Enthusiastic Earnestness, that's the term.

This Enthusiastic Earnestness has much emotion in it, it appeals to the Emotional side of human nature, rather than to the Thinking-Reasoning side. And yet an argument based upon reason and conducted upon logical principles, may be presented with Enthusiastic Earnestness with much greater effect than if the appeal to the reason is conducted in a cold, unemotional way. The average person is so constituted mentally that he thaws out under a manifestation of live, enthusiastic "feeling," under the term of Personal Magnetism. The "feeling" side of mentality is as important as the "thinking" side and it is far more common and universal, for the majority of people really think very little, while everyone "feels."

A writer in the "early seventies" of the last century said: "All of us emit a sphere, aura, or halo, impregnated with the very essence of ourselves; sensitives know it so do our dogs and other pets so does a hungry lion or tiger; aye, even flies, snakes, and the insects, as we know to our cost. Some of us are magnetic, others not. Some of us are warm, attractive, love inspiring and friendship making, while others are cold, intellectual, thoughtful, reasoning but not magnetic. Let a learned man of the latter type address an audience and it will soon tire of his intellectual discourse and will manifest symptoms of drowsiness. He talks at them but not into them, he makes them think, not feel, which is most tiresome to the majority of person's and few speakers succeed who attempt to merely make people think, they want to be made to feel. People will pay liberally to be made to feel or laugh, while they will begrudge a dime for instruction or talk that will make them think. Pitted against a learned man of the type mentioned above, let there be a half-educated, but very loving, ripe, and mellow man, with but nine-tenths of the logic and erudition of the first man, yet such a man carries along his crowd with perfect ease, and everybody is wide-awake, treasuring up every good thing that falls from his lips. The reasons are palpable and plain. It is heart against head; soul against logic; and is bound to win every time."

If you will notice the man and woman who are considered the most "magnetic," you will find that almost invariably they are people who have what is called "soul" about them that is, they manifest and induce "feeling," or emotion. They manifest traits of character and nature similar to that manifested by actors and actresses. They throw out a part of themselves, which seems to affect those coming in contact with them. Notice a non-magnetic actor, and you will see that although he may be letter perfect in his part, and may have acquired the proper mannerisms, gestures, and other technical parts of his art, still he lacks a "certain something," and that something may be seen to be the ability to communicate "feeling." Now, those who are in the secret know full well that many of the successful actors, who seem to burn with passion, feeling and emotion on the stage, really feel but little of these qualities while acting, they are like phonographs, giving off sounds that have been registered in them. But if you investigate still further, you will see that in studying their parts and practicing the same privately, these people induced a stimulated emotion, such as the part called for, and held it firmly in their minds, accompanying it with the appropriate gestures, etc., until it became firmly "set" there impressed upon the tablets of the mentality as the record of a phonograph is likewise impressed upon the wax. Then, when afterward they played the part, the outward semblance of the feelings, with the motions, gestures, emphasis, etc...., reproduced itself and impressed the audience. It is said that if an actor allows himself to be actually carried away with his part so that he feels the same keenly, the result will not be advantageous, for he is overcome with the feeling and its effect is upon himself rather than upon his audience. The best result is said to be obtained when one has first experienced and felt the emotion and then afterward reproduces it in the manner above stated without allowing it to control him.

We mention the above facts for the use of those who do not naturally possess the faculty or quality of Personal magnetism to the required degree. Such people will find it to their advantage to endeavor to work up the desired feeling of Enthusiastic Earnestness, in private, fixing the mental impression by frequent private rehearsals and practice until it becomes registered in their "habit mind," to be reproduced upon occasions when needed. Be a good actor, that is the advice in such cases, and remember that frequent practice and private rehearsal makes a good actor. It is a far better thing to be able to induce feeling and enthusiasm in this way, rather than be lacking it, on the one hand; or to be an "emotional inebriate" on the other hand. One may be rationally Enthusiastically Earnest, without being filled full of "slushy gush" or maudlin emotionalism. We think that the careful student will see just what is meant here and will not misunderstand us. And remember, that through this repeated "acting" the desired quality will often become real and "natural."

LESSON IX

Attractive Personality

How to acquire an Attractive Personality. The Charm of Personality. The quality of Self-Respect, Confidence and Mastery, What it does for one, and Develops its Personal qualities and traits that make for success, and how to acquire them.

We have explained in our lesson on "Individuality" that what is known, as the "Personality" was not the real "I" of the Individual but that instead it formed the "Me"

part of oneself, the outward appearance of the Individual. As we have told you, the word Personality really means the "mask" aspect of the Individual, the outward appearance of the part in the great drama of life that he is playing. And just as the actor may change his mask and costume, so may the Individual change, alter and replace his Personality by other features found desirable.

But nevertheless, while the Personality is not the real "I," it plays an important part in the drama of life, particularly as the audience pays more attention to the Personality, as a rule, than it does to the real Individual behind the mask. And so, it is proper that every Individual should cultivate and acquire a Personality that will prove attractive to his audience and render him acceptable to them. No, we are not preaching deception we regard Individuality as the Real Self and believe that one should build himself up to his highest and best according to the laws of Individual Unfoldment but, nevertheless, so long as one must wear a Personality about him as he goes through life, we believe that it is not only to his advantage but is also his duty to make that Personality as pleasing and attractive as he is able to. You know that no matter how good, intelligent and high-minded a man may be, if he wears the mask of an unattractive and unpleasant Personality he is placed at a disadvantage and drives away people whom he might benefit and who would be glad to love him if they could see behind his unattractive mask.

Nor are we speaking of one's personal physical appearance when we speak of unattractive and attractive masks. While one's physical appearance goes a good way in some cases, there is a charm of Personality that far transcends that fleeting appearance. There are many persons having beautiful faces and forms whose personality is far from charming, and who repel rather than attract. And there are others whose faces are homely and whose forms are far from shapely, who have, nevertheless, that "winning way about them" that attracts others to them. There are people whom we are always glad to see, and whose charm of manner makes us forget that they are not beautiful, in fact, even their homely faces seem to become transfigured when we are in their presence. That is what we meant by Personality, in the same way in which we are now using it. It bears a very close relationship to "Personal Magnetism," of which we spoke of in our preceding lesson.

One of the first things that should be cultivated by those wishing to develop the Charm of Personality is a mental atmosphere of Cheerfulness. There is nothing so invigorating as the presence of a cheerful person, nothing so dispiriting as one of those Human Wet Blankets that cast a chill over everyone and everything with whom they come in contact. Think of your acquaintances and you will find that you will naturally place them in two classes, the Cheerful ones, and the Gloomy ones. Sunny Jim is always preferred to Gloomy Gus, the one you will welcome and the other you will fly from. The Japanese understand this law of Personality, and one of the first things that they teach their children is to preserve a cheerful, sunny exterior, no matter if their hearts are breaking. With them it is considered one of the most flagrant offenses against good form to carry their sorrows, grief, and pain into the presence of others. They reserve that side of their life for the privacy of their own chamber to the outside world and they present always a happy, sunny smile. And in this they are wise, for a number of reasons

(1) that they may induce a more buoyant and positive state of mind in themselves,

(2) that they may attract cheerful persons and things to them by the Law of Attraction and

(3) that they may present an attractive Personality to others and thereby be welcome and congenial associates and participants in the work of life. There is little welcome or help for the Gloomy Gus tribe in everyday business life, they are avoided as a pestilence everyone has troubles enough of his own without those of other people added thereto. Remember the old lines:

"Laugh and the world laughs with you,
Weep and you weep alone.
For this sad old earth is in need of mirth,
And, has troubles enough of its own."

So, cultivate the Smile that Won't Come Off. It is a valuable asset of Personality. Not the silly, idiotic grin, but the Smile that means something, the Real Thing. And such a smile comes from within and is more than skin deep. If you want a Verbal Pattern upon which to model the mental state that will produce this outward appearance of Personality, here it is: "Bright, Cheerful and Happy." Frame it and hang it in a prominent place in your Mental Art Gallery. Commit it to memory and Visualize it, so that you may be able to see it before you like an illuminated electric sign "Bright, Cheerful and Happy." then endeavor to make the idea into reality within your mind. Think it out, act it out and it will become real to you. Then will you have Something

Worthwhile in the shape of Personality? This may seem simple and childish to you but, if you will work it out into actuality, it will be worth thousands of dollars to you, no matter what walk of life you may be in.

Another valuable bit of Personality is that of Self Respect. If you have real Self Respect, it will manifest itself in your outward demeanor and appearance. If you don't have it, you had better start in and cultivate the appearance of Self Respect, and then Remember that you are a Man or a Woman, as the case may be, and not a poor, crawling Worm on the Dust of a Human Door Mat. Face the world firmly and fearlessly, keeping your eyes well to the front. Hold up your head! There is nothing like a stiff backbone and a raised head for meeting the world. The man with bent head seems to apologize for living and being on the earth and the world is apt to take such at their own valuation. An erect head enables one to walk past the dragons at the door of Success. A writer gives the following good advice on this subject: "Hold your ear lobes directly over your shoulders, so that a plumb line hung from the ears describes the line of your body. Be sure also not to carry the head either to the right or left but vertical. Many men make the mistake, especially while waiting for a customer to finish some important piece of business, of leaning the head to the right or left. This indicates weakness. A study of men discloses the fact that the strong men never tilt the head. Their heads sit perfectly straight on strong necks. Their shoulders, held easily, yet firmly, in position, are inspiring in their strength indicating poise. Every line of the body, in other words, denotes the thought of the bearer." The value of this advice lies not only in the fact that it gives to you the "appearance" of Self Respect (no trifling matter, by the way), but also that it tends to cultivate a corresponding mental state within you. For just as "Thought takes form in Action," so do Actions develop mental states, it is a rule that works both ways. So, think Self Respect and act Self Respect. Let the "I Am" within you manifest itself. Don't crawl don't cringe, don't grovel but do be a Real Human Being.

Another bit of Personality worth cultivating is the Art of Taking an Interest in Others. Many people go through the world so wrapped up in their own affairs that they convey the impression of being "apart" and aloof from others with whom they come in contact. This mental state manifests in a most unpleasant form of Personality. Such people are not only regarded as "cold" and lacking heart and soul, but they also give others the impression of selfishness and hardness, and the public is apt to let such a person alone leave him to his own selfish moods and mental states. Such a one never becomes popular, never becomes a good mixer among men. Taking an Interest in Others is an art that well repays the student of Success to cultivate it. Of course, one must always keep the main chance before him and not allow one's own interests to suffer by reason of his interest in others that goes without saying, for unreasonable altruism is just as one sided as undue selfishness. But there is a middle course. You will find something of interest in every person with whom you come in contact, and if you will but turn your attention to that interest it will manifest itself in such a way that the person will be conscious of it will appreciate it and will be glad to respond by taking an interest in you. This is not deceit, or time serving, or flattery, it is the Law of Compensation working on the mental plane, you get what you give. If you will stop and think a moment you will find that the people, whose Personality seems the most attractive to you are the people who seem to Take an Interest in your own personality.

This Taking an Interest in Others manifests itself in many ways, one of which is in making you a Good Listener. Now, we do not mean that you should allow yourself to be made a dumping ground for all the talk of all the people with whom you come in contact, if you do this you will have time for nothing else. You must use ordinary judgment and tact in regulating the time you give to others, depending upon the person and the particular circumstances of the case. What we do mean is that while you're listening you should Listen Well. There is no subtler compliment that one person can pay to another than Listening Well to him or her. To Listen Well is to Listen with Interest. And that is something that cannot be very well taught in a book. Perhaps the best way to express the idea is to say, "Listen as you

Would be Listened unto." The Golden Rule may be applied to many things and ideas, with benefit and good results. The man who listens well is well thought of by those to whom he listens. In this connection we are always reminded of the old story of Carlyle, who, as everyone knows, was reputed to be a crusty, crabby old chap, prone to sarcastic remarks and brusque treatment of those with whom he engaged in conversation. The tale goes that one day a man called upon Carlyle and the man understood the Art of Listening Well. He turned the conversations so as to get Carlyle started on a subject dear to his heart and then he kept quiet and Listened Well. Carlyle talked "a straight streak" for several hours and grew quite enthusiastic over his topic. When at last the visitor arose to depart, he was forced to actually tear himself away from Carlyle, who, following him to the door, manifested unusual enthusiasm and good spirits and bidding him good-bye, said warmly: "Come again, mon come again and often—ye have a wonderfully bright mind, and I've enjoyed your conversation very much indeed—ye are a most delightful conversationalist."

Be careful not to bore people with your personal experiences better forget your personal self in talking to others except when it is right to the point to bring yourself in. People do not want to hear what a wonderful fellow you are, they want to tell you what wonderful people they are, which is very much more pleasant to them. Don't retail your woes, nor recite your many points of excellence. Don't tell what a wonderful baby you the other people have, have babies of their own to think about. You must endeavor to talk about things of interest to the other person if he wants to do the talking himself. Forget yourself and Take an Interest in the Other Person.

Some of the best retail merchants impress upon their salespeople the advantage of cultivating the mental attitude and personality that you will give the customer the impression that you are "on his side of the counter" that is that you are taking a personal interest in his being well-served, suited, well-treated, and satisfied. The salesman who is able to create that impression is well advanced on the road to success in his particular line. This is a difficult thing to describe, but a little observation and thought and practice along the lines laid down in the preceding lessons will do much for you in this direction. A recent writer truthfully says on this subject: "Suppose, for instance, you are in trade or a profession and wish to increase your business. It will not do, when you sell goods or services, to make the matter a merely perfunctory transaction, taking the customer's money, giving him good value and letting him go away feeling that you have no interest in the matter beyond giving him a fair deal and profiting thereby. Unless he feels that you have a personal interest in him and his needs, and that you are honestly desirous to increase his welfare, you have made a failure and are losing ground. When you can make every customer feel that you are really trying to advance his interests as well as you own, your business will grow. It is not necessary to give premiums, or heavier weights, or better values than others give to accomplish this; it is done by putting life and interest into every transaction, however small." This writer has stated the idea clearly, forcibly, and truthfully and you will do well to heed his advice and to put it into actual practice.

Another important point in Personality is Self-Control, particularly in the matter of Keeping your Temper. Anger is a mark of weakness, not of strength. The man who loses his temper immediately places himself at a disadvantage.

Remember the old saying: "Those whom the gods would destroy, they first make angry." Under the influence of anger, a man does all sorts of foolish things that he afterwards regrets. He throws judgment, experience and caution to the winds and acts like a crazy man. In fact, anger is a sort of madness, a phase of insanity, if you doubt this look carefully at the face of the first angry man you meet and see how irrational he looks and acts. It is a well-known fact that if one keeps cool while his opponent is angry, he has decidedly the best of the matter for he is a sane man dealing with an irrational one. It is the better policy to allow the other fellow to "stew in his own fat" of anger, keeping cool yourself at the same time. It is a comparatively easy matter to cool down an angry man without becoming angry with you and as it takes two to make a quarrel, the matter is soon over.

You will find that control of the outward expression will give you control of your inner mental state. You will find that if you are able to control your voice, keeping it calm, steady and low-pitched, you will not fly into a passion, and more than this, you will find by so doing that the voice of the other fellow will gradually come down from its loud, boisterous tones, and in the end both of you will be pitching your voices in the same key and you have set that keynote. This is worth remembering, this control of the voice it is a secret well worth knowing and practicing.

While we are on the subject of voice, we would like to call your attention to a further control of voice, or rather a cultivation of voice. A man having a well-controlled, even, pleasant voice has an advantage over others having equal abilities in other directions but lacking that one quality. The value of a vibrant, resonant, soft, and flexible voice is great. If you have such a voice, you are blessed. If you lack it, why start to work, and cultivate it. Oh, yes, you can! Did you ever hear of Nathan Sheppard, the well-known public speaker? Then listen to these words of his, telling of his natural disadvantages of voice, and how he overcame them and became a great speaker. He says: "When I made up my mind to devote my mind and body to public speaking, I was told by my teachers and governors that I would certainly fail; that my articulation was a failure, and it was that my organs of speech were inadequate, and they were and that if I would screw up my little mouth it could be put into my mother's thimble, and it could. Stinging words these certainly were, and cruel ones. I shall never forget them; possibly, however, they stung me into a persistency that I would have never known but for these words. At all events, that is the philosophy of the 'self-made' world of mankind. I may not have accomplished much, but I do not claim to have accomplished much. It is something I have made a living out of, my art for twenty years and that I do claim to have done in spite of every obstacle and every discouragement, by turning my will upon my voice and vocal organs, by cultivating my elocutionary instincts and my ear for the cadences of rhetoric, by knowing what I and my voice and my feelings were about, by making the most of myself." After these words, anything that we might add regarding the possibility of acquiring a good voice by will, practice and desire would be superfluous. Pick out the kind of voice that you think is best adapted to your work and then cultivate it by practice, determination, and desire. If Mr. Sheppard could become a famous public speaker with such obstacles as these, then for you to say "but I can't" is to stamp you as a weakling.

It has been suggested to us that we have a few words to say regarding the carriage or physical bearing of the person, as an important part of Personality particularly in the phase of Walking. But we do not think that is necessary to add to what we have said in this lesson regarding the subject, in connection with what we have also said regarding the mental state of Self Respect. The main thing is to cultivate the Mental State of Self Respect and the rest will follow as a natural consequence. Thought takes form in Action, and the man who has Self Respect imbedded in his mind will surely so carry and demean him that he will give evidence of his mental state in his every physical action, gesture, carriage, and motion. He must have it within, as well as without. One must pay attention to the exterior aspect of course, particularly in the matter of dress. One should cultivate Cleanliness and Neatness, of both body and clothing. To be well dressed does not mean to me showily clad, in fact, the person who is best dressed is inconspicuously dressed. Cultivate a quiet, refined taste, expressed in quality rather than in showiness. And above all be Clean.

In conclusion, let us impress upon you again and again that that which we call Personality is but the outer mask of the Individual Within. The mask may be changed by an effort of the Will, aided by an intelligent discrimination. First find out what kind of Personality you should have, and then set to work to cultivate it to grow it, in fact. From the Mental Image of what you want to be then think of it, desire it ardently will that you shall have it then Act It Out, over and over again rehearsal after rehearsal, until you will actually materialize your ideal into objective reality. Make a good mental pattern or mold, and then pour in your mental material steadily, and slowly! From the mold will come forth the Character and Personality that you desire and need. Then polish up this newborn Personality until it becomes radiant with the brightness of Culture.

You can be what you want to be if you only want to be hard enough. Desire is the mother of the Actuality. Remember once more the old rule, Earnest Desire, Confident Expectation, Firm Resolve these are the three things that lead to Accomplishment.

And now that we have given you this little Secret of Success Use It. "It is Up to You" to "Make Good." We have "pressed the button, you must do the rest!"

An Afterword

On reading the foregoing pages after they have been set up in type, we are impressed with the idea that in spite of our determination, as expressed in the first few

pages, not to attempt to lay down a code of rules or a course of conduct which should be considered as an infallible Guide to Success in spite of our vowed determination not to pose as a teacher or preacher, we have nevertheless managed to do considerable in the direction of "laying down the law" so far as is concerned naming of things to be done or avoided.

However, we feel that the advice given is good and that the various examples quoted are calculated to arouse within the mind of the reader the Spirit that leads to Success. And, with this thought, we send forth these pages to those who may attract them to themselves, or who may be attracted to them, under the Law of Attraction.

But we feel that we shall not have completed our task unless we, once more, remind the reader that Success is not to be gained by a blind and slavish following of anyone's rules or advice, our own any more than any other persons. There is no Royal Road to Success, no Patent Process by which the unsuccessful are to be magically transformed into Captains of Industry or Magnates of Wall Street. There is nothing more amusing, or pitiful, according to how one views it than the bulk of Success Talk given to the public by self-appointed teachers and preachers. There is no one who can in a few pages point out to seekers after Success an infallible method whereby each and every one may attain the Success and Attainment that their hearts crave. It is a cold, hard truth that each and every man must work out his own salvation in the matter of Success. Rules and advice may greatly assist, and they undoubtedly do this, but the individual must accomplish the real work. He must carve out his own Destiny, and there is no power above or below that will do the work for him if he refuses to perform it himself.

The old saying that "God helps him who helps himself" is true in more senses than one. It is true in the sense that Higher Aid seems to refuse to come to the assistance of one who is not willing to strike out for him and do his best. But it is true in another sense, this Aid does come to one who will throw heart and soul into the task set before him, and who will do each day's work the best he know how, with hope in his soul and a confident expectation of better things right ahead around the turn of the road. The wise man is the one who takes courageously the step right ahead of him, planting his foot firmly and confidently upon it, although he is unable to see further ahead. To such a one- step after step is illuminated as he proceeds, and he reaches his goal, whereas the shrinking ones, who have feared to take the obvious step because they could not see beyond it, are still waiting for something to turn up. This waiting business is a poor policy as Garfield said: "Don't wait for something to turn up, go out and turn something up." Take the step before you boldly and hopefully and the next step will then appear. The thing to do is what lies right before you to be done, do it the best you know how, feeling assured that in it's doing you will be making progress toward the better things for which your heart has been longing. New ideas come while you are in action, in the doing of things comes the inspiration for the doing of greater things. You can always get a better "running start" when in action, which will give you an advantage over the best "standing start" imaginable. Get into action and motion.

In this little work we have endeavored to call your attention to something of far greater importance than a mere code of rules and general advice. We have pointed out to you the glorious fact that within each of you there is a Something Within, which if once aroused would give you a greatly increased power and capacity. And so, we have tried to tell you this story of the Something Within, from different viewpoints, so that you might catch the idea in several ways. We firmly believe that Success depends most materially upon a recognition and manifestation of this Something Within, we think that a study of the character and work of all successful men will show you that differ as they do in personal characteristics, they all manifest that consciousness of that Something Within them that gives them an assurance of Inward Power and Strength, from which proceeds Courage and Self-Confidence. You will find that the majority of successful men feel that there is a Something helping them back of and behind their efforts. Some have called this Thing by the name of "Luck" or "Destiny," or some such term. But it is all a form of the same recognition of an Inward Power that they are "helped" in some way, although they are not quite sure of the nature of the helper in fact, the majority of them do not stop to speculate upon its nature, they are too busy and are content with the knowledge that It is there. This Something Within is the Individual the "I" in each of them, the source of the power which men manifest when they express it. And this little book is written in the hopes that to many it may be the first step toward the recognition, unfoldment, and manifestation of this Inward Power.

We earnestly urge upon you to cultivate this, "I Am" consciousness that you may realize the Power Within you. And then there will come naturally to you the correlated consciousness which expresses itself in the statement, "I Can, and I Will," one of the grandest affirmations of Power that man can make. This "I Can, and I Will" consciousness is that expression of the Something Within, which we trust that you will realize and manifest. We feel that behind all the advice that we can give you, this one thing is the Prime Factor in the Secret of Success.

LIST OF TITLES WITH ISBN NO.

ISBN	TITLE
9788194914129	1984
9789390575220	1984 & Animal Farm (2In1)
9789390575572	1984 & Animal Farm (2In1): The International Best-Selling Classics
9789390575848	35 Sonnets
9789390575329	A Clergyman's Daughter
9789390575923	A Study In Scarlet
9789390896097	A Tale Of Two Cities
9789390896837	Abide in Christ
9789390896202	Abraham Lincoln
9789390896912	Absolute Surrender
9789390896608	African American Classic Collection
9789390575305	Aldous Huxley: The Collected Works
9789390896141	An Autobiography of M. K. Gandhi
9789390575886	Animal Farm
9789390575619	Animal Farm & The Great Gatsby (2In1)
9789390575626	Animal Farm & We
9789390896158	Anna Karenina
9789390575534	Antic Hay
9789390896165	Antony & Cleopatra
9789390896172	As I Lay Dying
9789390896226	As You like it
9789390575671	At Your Command
9789390575350	Awakened Imagination
9789390575114	Be What You Wish
9789390896233	Believe In yourself
9789390896998	Best of Charles Darwin: The Origin of Species & Autobiography
9789390896684	Best Of Horror : Dracula And Frankenstein
9789390575503	Best Of Mark Twain (The Adventures of Tom Sawyer AND The Adventures of Huckleberry Finn)
9789390896769	Black History Collection
9789390575756	Brave New World, Animal Farm & 1984 (3in1)

9789390896240	Brother Karamzov
9789390575053	Bulleh Shah Poetry
9789390575725	Burmese Days
9789390896257	Bushido
9789390896066	Can't Hurt Me
9788194914112	Chanakya Neeti: With The Complete Sutras
9789390896042	Crime and Punishment
9789390575527	Crome Yellow
9789390575046	Down and Out in Paris and London
9789390896844	Dracula
9789390575442	Emersons Essays: The Complete First & Second Series (Self-Reliance & Other Essays)
9789390575749	Emma
9789390575817	Essential Tozer Collection - The Pursuit of God & The Purpose of Man
9789390896578	Fascism What It Is and How to Fight It
9789390575688	Feeling is the Secret
9789390575190	Five Lessons
9789390575954	Frankenstein
9789390575237	Franz Kafka: Collected Works
9789390575282	Franz Kafka: Short Stories
9789390575060	George Orwell Collected Works
9789390575077	George Orwell Essays
9789390575213	George Orwell Poems
9788194914150	Greatest Poetry Ever Written Vol 1
9788194914143	Greatest Poetry Ever Written Vol 1
9789390896301	Gulliver's Travel
9789390575961	Gunaho Ka Devta
9789390575893	H. P. Lovecraft Selected Stories Vol 1
9789390575978	H. P. Lovecraft Selected Stories Vol 2
9789390896059	Hamlet
9789390575022	His Last Bow: Some Reminiscences of Sherlock Holmes
9789390896134	History of Western Philosophy
9789390575121	Homage To Catalonia

9789390896219	How to develop self-confidence and Improve public Speaking
9789390896295	How to enjoy your life and your Job
9789390575633	How to own your own mind
9789390896318	How to read Human Nature
9789390896325	How to sell your way through the life
9789390896370	How to use the laws of mind
9789390896387	How to use the power of prayer
9789390896028	How to win friends & Influence People
9788194824176	How To Win Friends and Influence People
9789390896103	Humility The Beauty of Holiness
9789390896653	Imperialism the Highest Stage of Capitalism
9789390575084	In Our Time
9789390575169	In Our Time & Three Stories and Ten poems
9789390575145	James Allen: The Collected Works
9789390896189	Jesus Himself
9789390575480	Jo's Boys
9789390896394	Julius Caesar
9789390575404	Keep the Aspidistra Flying
9789390896400	Kidnapped
9789390896424	King Lear
9789390575824	Lady Susan
9789390896455	Law of Success
9789390896264	Lincoln The Unknown
9789390575565	Little Men
9789390575640	Little Women
9788194914174	Lost Horizon
9789390896462	Macbeth
9789390896929	Man Eaters of Kumaon
9789390896523	Man The Dwelling Place of God
9789390896349	Man The Dwelling Place of God
9789390575909	Mansfield Park
9788194914136	Manto Ki 25 Sarvshreshth Kahaniya
9789390896509	Marxism, Anarchism, Communism
9789390575664	Mathematical Principles of Natural Philosophy

9788194914198	Meditations
9789390575800	Mein Kampf
9789390575794	Memory How To Develop, Train, And Use It
9789390896486	Mind Power
9789390896585	Money
9789390575039	Mortal Coils
9789390575770	My Life and Work
9789390896035	Narrative of the Life of Frederick Douglass
9789390575152	Neville Goddard: The Collected Works
9789390575985	Northanger Abbey
9789390896530	Notes From Underground
9789390896547	Oliver Twist
9789390575459	On War
9789390575541	One, None and a Hundred Thousand
9789390896554	Othelo
9789390575435	Out Of This World
9789390575015	Persuasion
9789390575510	Prayer The Art Of Believing
9789390575091	Pride and Prejudice
9789390896561	Psychic Perception
9789390575381	Rabindranath Tagore - 5 Best Short Stories Vol 2
9789390575367	Rabindranath Tagore - Short Stories (Masters Collections Including The Childs Return)
9789390575374	Rabindranath Tagore 5 Best Short Stories Vol 1 (Including The Childs Return
9789390896622	Romeo & Juliet
9789390896127	Sanatana Dharma
9789390575596	Seedtime & Harvest
9789390896639	Selected Stories of Guy De Maupassant
9789390575206	Self-Reliance & Other Essays
9789390575176	Sense and Sensibility
9789390575299	Shyamchi Aai
9789390896738	Socialism Utopian and Scientific
9789390896646	Success Through a Positive Mental Attitude
9789390575428	The Adventures of Huckleberry Finn

9789390575183	The Adventures of Sherlock Holmes
9789390575343	The Adventures of Tom Sawyer
9789390896691	The Alchemy Of Happiness
9789390575862	The Art Of Public Speaking
9789390896288	The Autobiography Of Charles Darwin
9788194914181	The Best of Franz Kafka: The Metamorphosis & The Trial
9789390575008	The Call Of Cthulhu and Other Weird Tales
9789390575107	The Case-Book of Sherlock Holmes
9789390896110	The Castle Of Otranto
9789390896745	The Communist Manifesto
9789390575589	The Complete Fiction of H. P. Lovecraft
9789390575497	The Complete Works of Florence Scovel Shinn
9789390896820	The Conquest of Breard
9789390896813	The Diary of a Young Girl
9789390896332	The Diary of a Young Girl The Definitive Edition of the Worlds Most Famous Diary
9789390575701	The Great Gatsby, Animal Farm & 1984 (3In1)
9789390575312	The Greatest Works Of George Orwell (5 Books) Including 1984 & Non-Fiction
9789390575992	The Hound of Baskervilles
9789390896707	The Idiot
9789390896714	The Invisible Man
9789390575657	The Knowledge of the holy
9789390575558	The Law & the Promise
9789390896721	The Law Of Attraction
9789390896776	The Leader in you
9789390896363	The Life of Christ
9789390896196	The Man-Eating Leopard of Rudraprayag
9789390896783	The Master Key to Riches
9789390575268	The Memoirs Of Sherlock Holmes
9789390896479	The Midsummer Night's Dream
9789390575466	The Mill On The Floss
9789390896790	The Miracles of your mind
9789390896660	The Mutual Aid A Factor in Evolution
9789390896448	The Origin of Species

9789390896905	The Peter Kropotkin Anthology The Conquest of Bread & Mutual Aid A Factor of Evolution
9789390896806	The Picture of Dorian Gray
9789390896271	The Picture of Dorian Gray
9789390575275	The Power Of Awareness
9789390896356	The Power of Concentration
9788194824169	The Power of Positive Thinking
9789390575411	The Power of the Spoken Word
9788194914105	The Power Of Your Subconscious Mind
9789390896899	The Power of Your Subconscious Mind
9789390896417	The Principles of Communism
9789390575787	The Psychology Of Mans Possible Evolution
9789390896615	The Psychology of Salesmanship
9789390575732	The Pursuit of God
9789390575398	The Pursuit of Happiness
9789390896851	The Quick and Easy Way to effective Speaking
9789390575947	The Return Of Sherlock Holmes
9789390575138	The Road To Wigan Pier
9789390896981	The Root of the Righteous
9789390575855	The Science Of Being Well
9788194914167	The Science Of Getting Rich, The Science Of Being Great & The Science Of Being Well (3In1)
9789390896011	The Screwtape Letters
9789390896073	The Screwtape Letters
9789390575336	The Secret Door to Success
9789390575695	The Secret Of Imagining
9789390896868	The Secret Of Success
9789390896431	The Seven Last Words
9789390575930	The Sign of the Four
9789390896004	The Sonnets
9789390896516	The Souls of Black Folk
9789390896875	The Sound and The Fury
9789390575244	The State and Revolution
9789390896882	The Story of My Life
9789390896936	The Story Of Oriental Philosophy

9789390896752	The Strange Case of Dr. Jekyll and Mr. Hyde
9789390896943	The Tempest
9789390575916	The Valley Of Fear
9789390575879	The Wind in the willows
9789390896080	The Wind in the willows
9789390575763	Their eyes were watching gofd
9789390575831	Three Stories
9789390896950	Twelfth Night
9789390896592	Twelve Years a Slave
9789390896677	Up from Slavery
9789390896974	Value Price and Profit
9789390896967	Wake Up and Live
9789390896493	With Christ in the School of Prayer
9789390575602	Your Faith is Your Fortune
9789390575473	Your Infinite Power To Be Rich
9789390575251	Your Word is Your Wand
9789390575718	Youth
9789391316099	A Christmas Carol
9789391316105	A Doll's House
9789391316501	A Passage to India
9789391316709	A Portrait of the Artist as a Young Man
9789391316112	A Tale of Two Cities
9789391316747	A Tear and a Smile
9789391316167	Agnes Gray
9789391316174	Alice's Adventures in Wonderland
9789391316136	Anandamath
9789391316181	Anne Of Green Gables
9789391316754	Anthem
9789391316198	Around The World in 80 Days
9789391316013	As A Man Thinketh
9789391316242	Autobiography of a Yogi
9789391316266	Beyond Good and Evil
9789391316761	Bleak House
9789391316778	Chitra, a Play in One Act
9789391316310	David Copperfield

9789391316075	Demian
9789391316785	Dubliners
9789391316051	Favourite Tales from the Arabian Nights
9789391316235	Gitanjali
9789391316068	Gravity
9789391316150	Great Speeches of Abraham Lincoln
9789391316662	Guerilla Warfare
9789391316839	Kim
9789391316822	Mother
9789391316211	My Childhood
9789391316846	Nationalism
9789391316327	Oliver Twist
9789391316853	Pygmalion
9789391316334	Relativity: The Special and the General Theory
9789391316389	Scientific Healing Affirmation
9789391316341	Sons and Lovers
9789391316587	Tales from India
9789391316372	Tess of The D'Urbervilles
9789391316396	The Awakening and Selected Stories
9789391316402	The Bhagvad Gita
9789391316303	The Book of Enoch
9789391316228	The Canterville Ghost
9789391316907	The Dynamic Laws of Prosperity
9789391316006	The Great Gatsby
9789391316860	The Hungry Stones and Other Stories
9789391316433	The Idiot
9789391316440	The Importance of Being Earnest
9789391316297	The Light of Asia
9789391316914	The Madman His Parables and Poems
9789391316457	The Odyssey
9789391316921	The Picture of Dorian Gray
9789391316464	The Prince
9789391316938	The Prophet
9789391316945	The Republic
9789391316518	The Scarlet Letter

9789391316143	The Seven Laws of Teaching
9789391316525	The Story of My Experiments with Truth
9789391316532	The Tales of the Mother Goose
9789391316549	The Thirty Nine Steps
9789391316594	The Time Machine
9789391316600	The Turn of the Screw
9789391316983	The Upanishads
9789391316617	The Yellow Wallpaper
9789391316426	The Yoga Sutras of Patanjali
9789391316990	Ulysses
9789391316624	Utopia
9789391316679	Vanity Fair
9789391316020	What Is To Be Done
9789391316686	Within A Budding Grove
9789391316693	Women in Love